STECK-VAUGHN

NEW WAY

HEADS and TAILS

Things

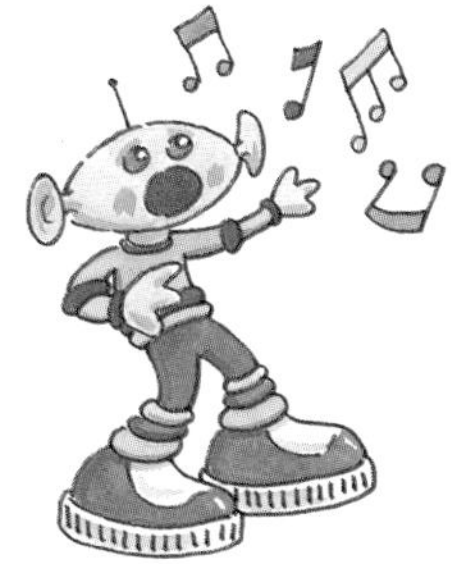

STECK-VAUGHN COMPANY

A Division of Harcourt Brace & Company

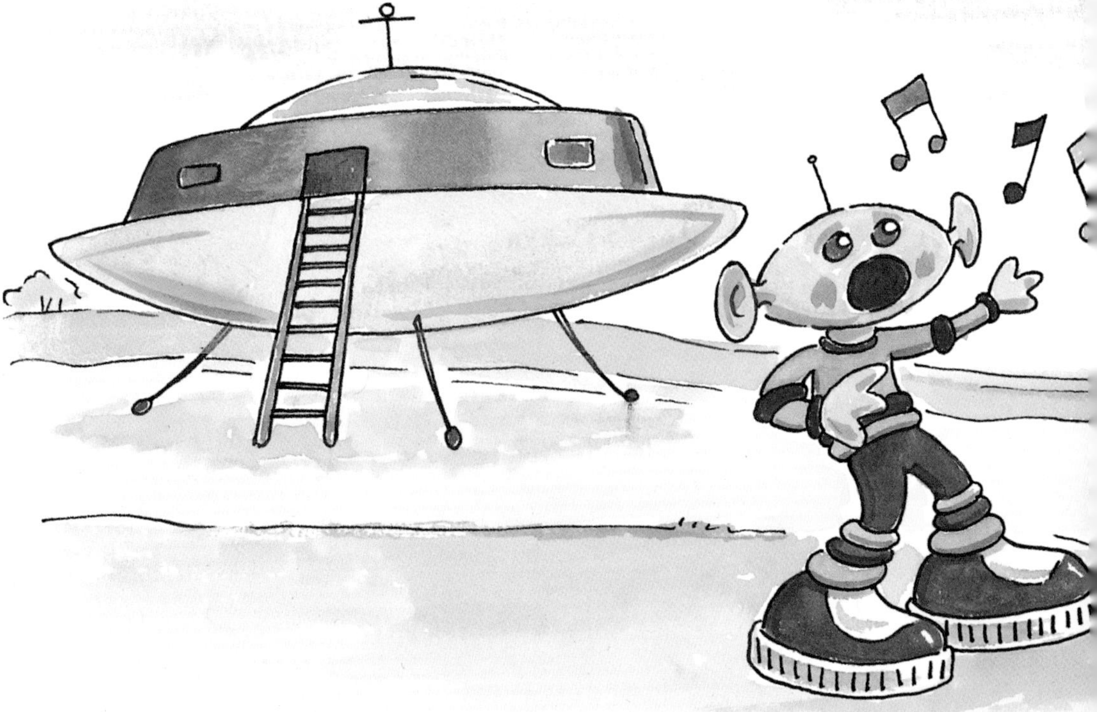

a singing thing

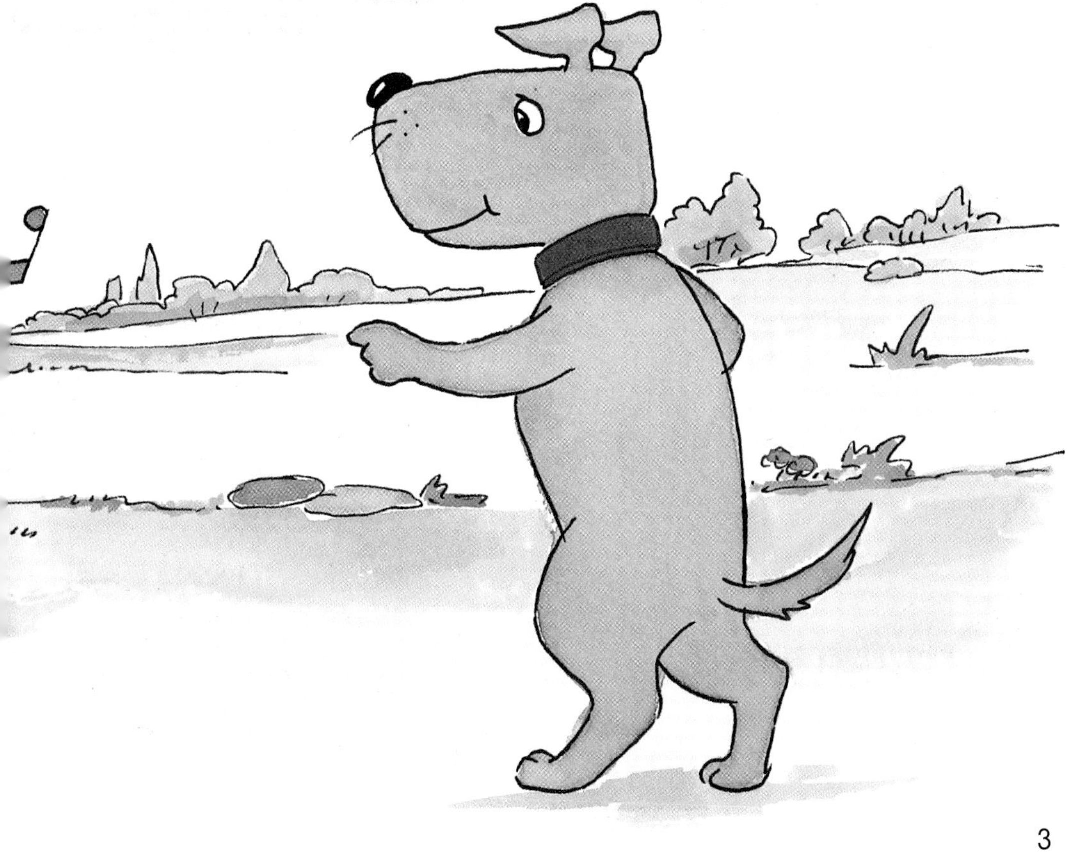

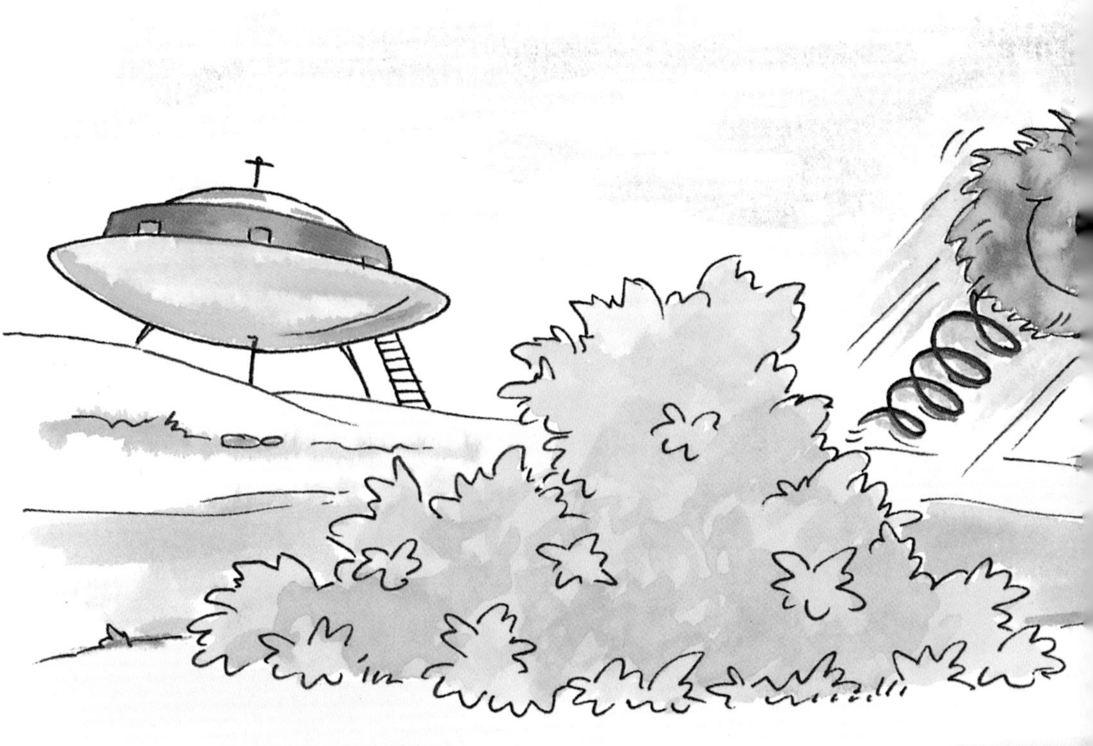

a springing thing

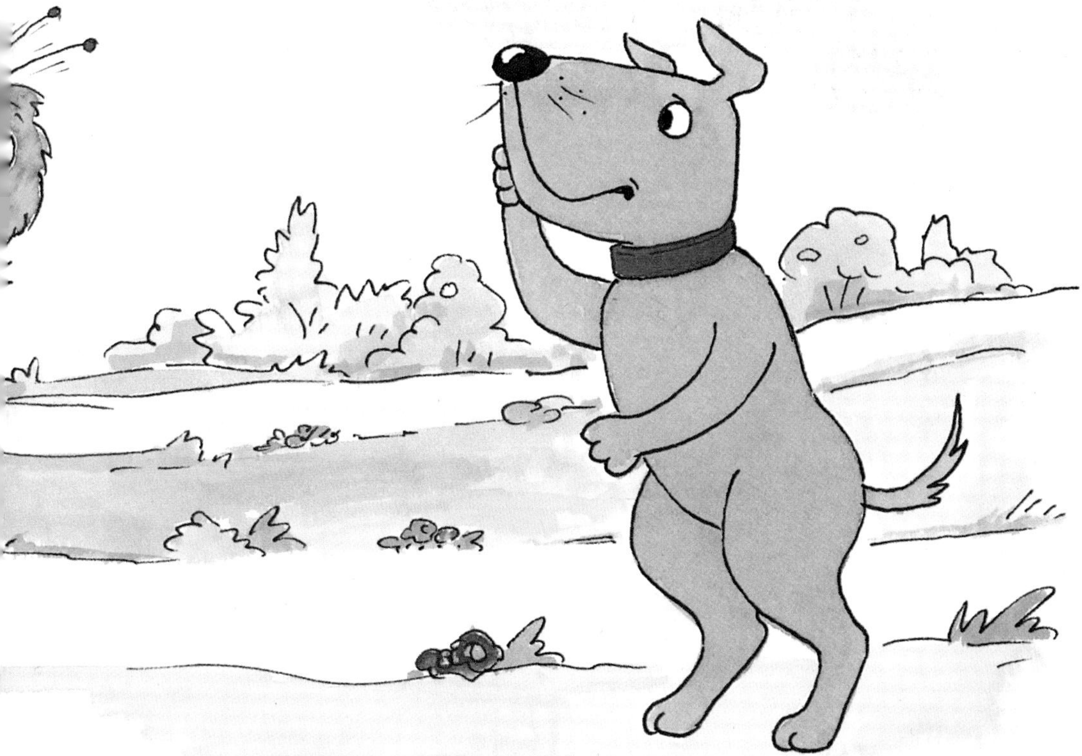

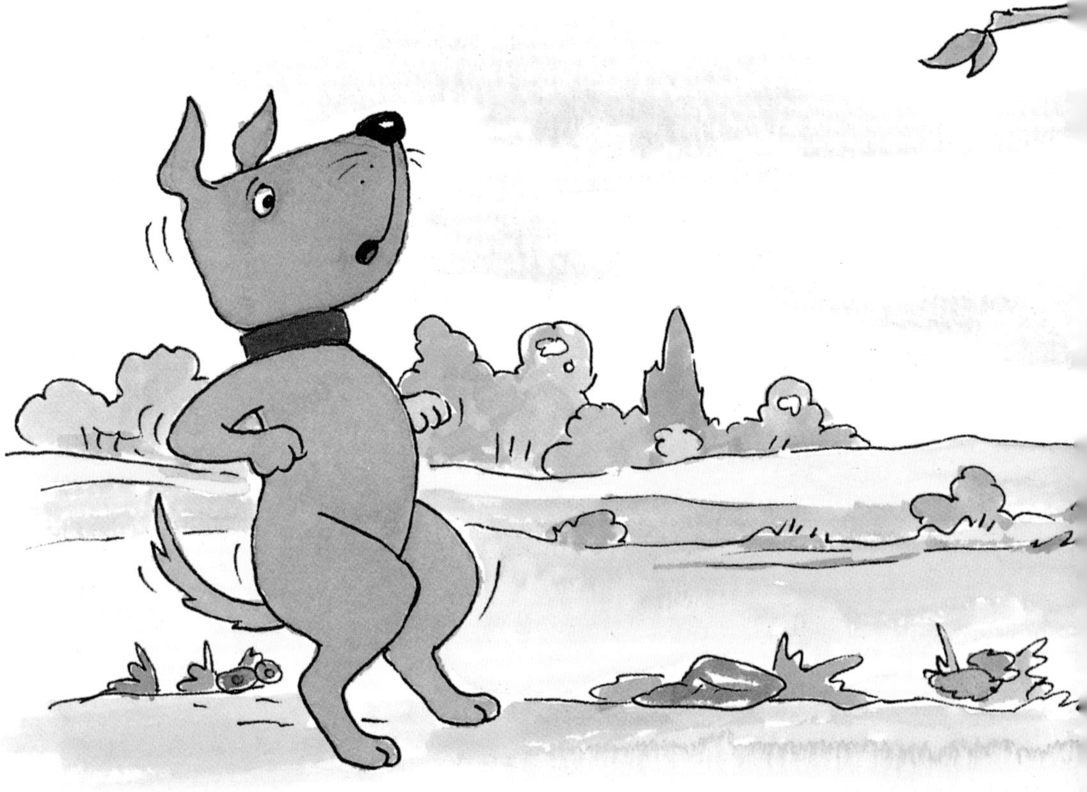

a swinging thing

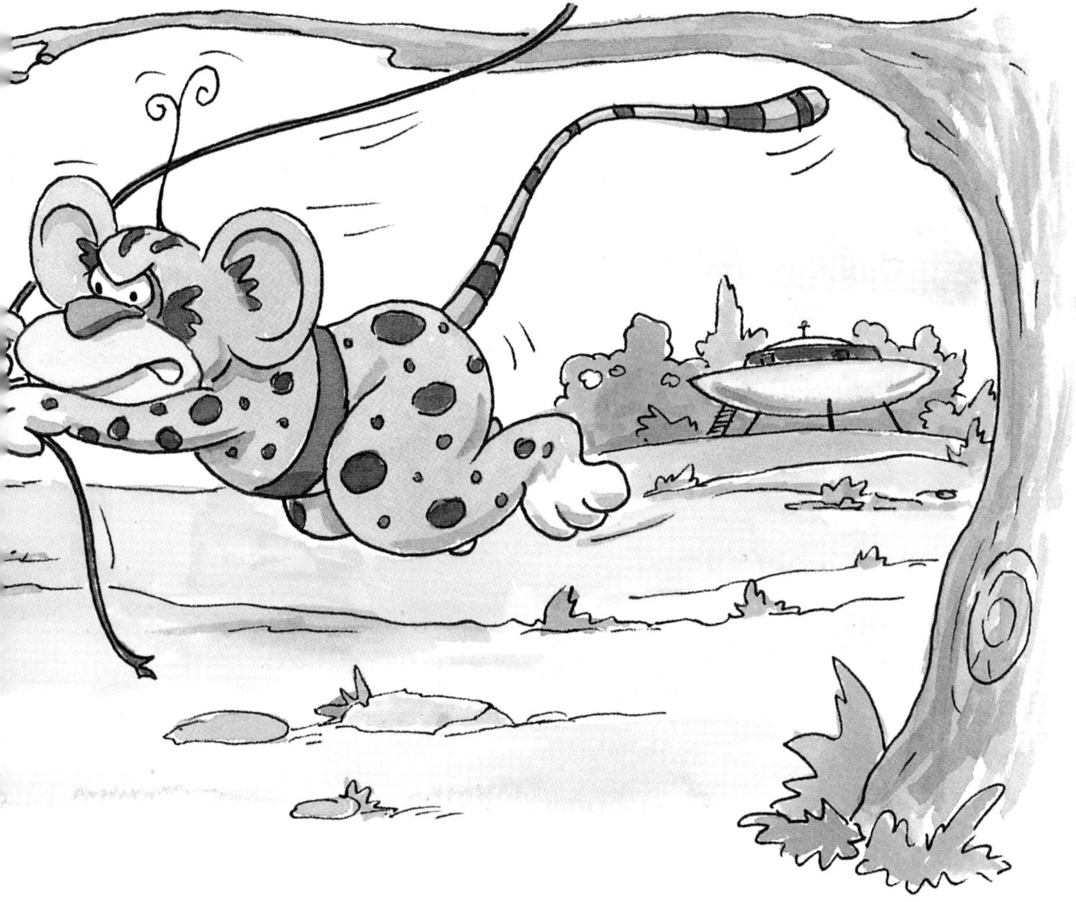

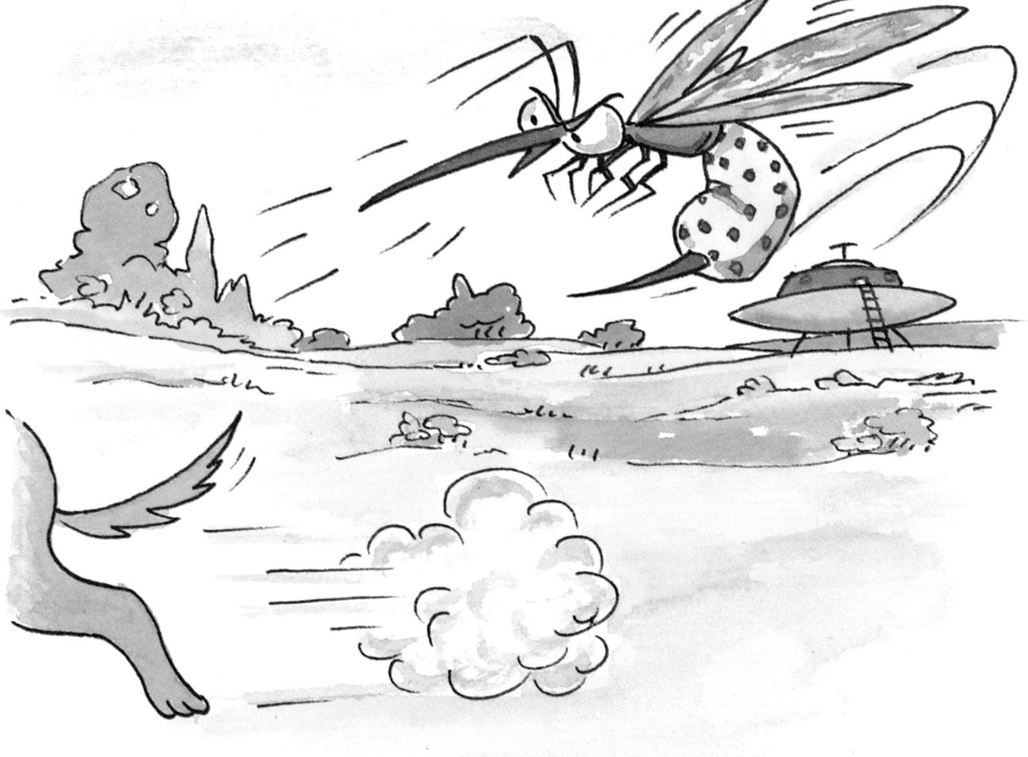

a stinging thing